WINDOWS ON OUR SOULS

WINDOWS ON OUR SOULS

art by Sarah Hall
text by Bob Shantz

Foreword by Peter Larisey, s.j.

NOVALIS

© 2007 Novalis, Saint Paul University, Ottawa, Canada

Cover design and layout: Audrey Wells
Art by Sarah Hall

Business Office:
Novalis Publishing Inc.
10 Lower Spadina Ave., Suite 400
Toronto, Ontario, Canada
M5V 2Z2

Novalis Publishing Inc.
4475 Frontenac Street
Montreal, Quebec, Canada
H2H 2S2

Phone: 1-800-387-7164
Fax: 1-800-204-4140
E-mail: books@novalis.ca
www.novalis.ca

Library and Archives Canada Cataloguing in Publication

Hall, Sarah, 1951–
    Windows on our souls / art by Sarah Hall ; text by Bob Shantz.

ISBN 978-2-89507-841-8

    1. Christian art and symbolism. 2. Devotional literature.
3. Catacombs–Italy–Rome.   I. Shantz, Bob, 1948–   II. Title.

BV4801.H24 2007   242   C2007-903241-9

Printed in Canada.

Interior images:
p. 12 – Erich Lessing / Art Resource, NY.
p. 13 – Pontificio Commissione de Archeologia Sacra in Rome. Reprinted by permission of the publisher from *The Catacombs: Life and Death in Early Christianity*, by James Stevenson (London: Thames and Hudson, 1978), p. 89.
p. 14 – Pontificio Commissione de Archeologia Sacra in Rome. Reprinted by permission of the publisher from *The Origins of Christian Art*, by Michael Gough (London: Thames and Hudson, 1973), p. 37.

We acknowledge the financial support of the Government of Canada through the Book Publishing Industry Development Program (BPIDP) for our publishing activities.

5   4   3   2   1   11   10   09   08   07

DEDICATIONS

The catacomb window images are dedicated to Jeffrey Kraegel. —Sarah Hall

My catacomb window reflections are dedicated to Alison in gratitude for her gifts of love and freedom.—Bob Shantz

ACKNOWLEDGMENTS

Special thanks to Fr. Vito Marziliano, for his steadfast support and mentoring of my stained glass projects over the years, and to Andre Beneteau, for his patient photography of my work.—Sarah Hall

I want to give a very special word of appreciation to Peter O'Brien for his superb editing, hearty encouragement and wise counsel. —Bob Shantz

CONTENTS

FOREWORD

On the Beginnings of Christian Art
and on the Breakthrough Generation
of Early Christians

by Peter Larisey, s.j.

I found visiting the Catacombs in Rome a fascinating experience, yet I was a bit spooked by the possibility of getting lost. There are hundreds of kilometres of them underneath what once were the outskirts of the ancient city. At several different sites, they were dug out in layers, one seemingly endless network below the other. Each catacomb has its own guides. These are absolutely necessary: one could so easily get lost in the labyrinthine darkness beyond the light from the few electric bulbs. I did lag behind one group I was with in the Catacomb of St. Priscilla, but not out of sight and not for long. A map of the Callistus catacomb reminds me of a spider's web, but a many-layered and unsystematic one.

To begin a catacomb tour, a visitor climbs down some stairs into a tunnel-like gallery and almost immediately senses the cool temperature. You also notice the small, triangular pick-marks left in the damp walls by those diggers – called *fossores* – of nearly two thousand years ago. Their prominence in the culture – they were also painters and managers – reflects the importance the Christian community placed on the obligation to bury the dead.

The Roman catacombs seem very far away from you and me in this already fast-moving 21st century. But to search back for them and their images can be enjoyable, and, in spite of that, it's also a helpful thing to do. That's because in helping us understand our beginnings, we get to know ourselves and our traditions better. To get our minds to consider them we must swim back through almost 20 rich centuries of Christian history and art. So why bother? One of the main reasons is that it is in the catacombs of the breakthrough generation that we find the very beginnings of Christian art. Our minds are populated with plenty of images from that vast tradition.

Before looking at the importance of the invention of Christian art by the breakthrough generation in those early Roman catacombs, it will be helpful to know something about their context. The vibrant Christian spirituality in the earlier centuries of the Church can be found not in painted or carved images but in the writings of the New Testament – the four Gospels, the Epistles of Paul, James, Peter and others, and the Book of Revelation. This collection, which nourishes us still, was complete around the year 100 CE. A burgeoning Christian spirituality is also embodied in the writings of the Apostolic Fathers, who came next. These included Hermas (second century), author of the "Shepherd," and the anonymous "Didache" (first or second century). Each of these included instructions for Christians on how to live. Pope St. Clement of Rome flourished around 96 CE. His First Epistle to the Corinthians deals with questions of stability of the ministry, obedience and the Eucharist. Early Christian spirituality is especially alive in the Epistles of St. Ignatius of Antioch (c. 35–c. 107 CE).

His Epistle to the Romans vibrates with his passionate love of Christ and his desire for martyrdom, which are expressed in powerful, imagistic writing.

Why was such spirituality expressed only in words? Why not in visual imagery? Looking further into the cultural context of the early Christians, I'd like to make a couple of observations. To begin with, the first Christians were Jews. They lived and prayed in the only culture they knew, which was centred in Jerusalem and the Temple. Given this tradition's prohibition of image making, it is not surprising that archeologists have so far found no Christian images or identifiable objects dating from the first Christian century.

What about the second century? Most of its hundred years were free of Christian imagery too. The reasons were different. Paul and the other apostles had been energetic in bringing the Good News of Jesus to the known world of the time, much of which was within the Roman Empire. An interesting document from the year 200 gives us a window on the attitudes of contemporary Christians to surrounding cultures. Written by an unidentified Christian, it was addressed to Diognetus, the Imperial Roman procurator of Egypt:

> Christians distinguish themselves from other people not by nationality or by language or by dress. They do not inhabit their own cities or use a special language or practice a life that makes them conspicuous…. They live in Greek and barbarian cities, following the lot that each has chosen, and they conform to indigenous customs in matters of clothing and food and the rest of life.[1]

---

[1]   Anonymous, quoted in Paul Corby Finney, *The Invisible God: The Earliest Christians on Art* (New York: Oxford University Press, 1994), 105.

Another illustration of Christian invisibility in Roman culture, by Clement of Alexandria (c. 150–c. 215), is about imagery. In a letter written also around 200, he advised Christians about the kind of image they should have on their signet rings, which were necessary for doing business or signing documents. Clement expects his readers to choose rings from supplies already made, findable on stone-cutters' shelves in any market. Believers were not to create specific Christian imagery. He suggests several possibilities: they could choose an image of a dove, an anchor, a fish, a ship, a lyre or a ship's anchor. But so could and did the non-Christian majority. Clement lists commonly available signet-ring imagery that should be avoided, such as swords and bows, "since we follow the path of peace," or drinking cups, "since we are sober."[2] In other words, Christians must adapt what is available in the culture that surrounds them, but be both inconspicuous and discriminating in their choices.

Every pagan, Jewish or Christian corpse in Rome had to be buried underground, not in an above-ground monument.[3] All burials had to be done outside the city walls, which is why we find the catacomb sites about three to five kilometres from the present city centre. The kilometres of underground burial galleries were possible because the deep soil was a substance called tufa, which is best understood as a soft rock. It was relatively easy to burrow through it, and because the tufa became dry and hard after being excavated, the top or roof of a structure or a single grave would not collapse.

---

[2] See Finney, 111.

[3] Pagans were more likely to cremate their dead and store the ashes in jars or urns and then bury them.

Many of the catacomb sites in Rome are associated with the burial place of a martyr. Thus we have the catacombs of Callistus, killed in 222; of Priscilla, martyred in the first century; of Sebastian, killed during the Diocletian Persecution, which began in 303; of St. Agnes, martyred we don't know when but long before her basilica was started in 350. Christians of the second century believed it was important to be buried near the martyrs because they could tag along when these proven friends of God would be among the first taken into the Resurrection. However, the Catacomb of Domitilla, begun about 150 and one of the largest in Rome, was named after St. Domitilla, who, the story goes, was a Christian and a niece of the Emperor Domitian (81–96). She was accused of "atheism and Jewish customs" and died in exile near the end of the first century. The catacomb uses her name because she had owned the land under which the first parts of the Catacomb of Domitilla were dug.[4]

Along the walls of an easily excavated gallery, horizontal burial places or loculi were dug out. Sometimes there were as many as five spaced between floor and ceiling. (Figure 1.)

Figure 1. Catacomb of St. Callistus: Gallery with loculi.

---

[4] See James Stevenson, *The Catacombs: Life and Death in Early Christianity* (London: Thames and Hudson, 1978), 27. "Atheism" would mean that she refused to worship the Emperor. Early Christians believed Domitilla was a Christian, but the catacomb is named after her because it was begun about 150 under property she had owned.

It is in such individual loculi that ordinary Romans and the poor would be buried. The loculi were often closed with pieces of stone, hardened clay fragments or bricks. Sometimes, if the surviving family had the means, a flat rectangular piece of marble would be used, with identifying information. For the Christians, after about 175, a symbolic picture – e.g., Noah and a dove with an olive branch – might be used. Many of these have been saved; I saw a number of them in the Vatican's Pio Christian Museum.

But the catacomb paintings, where do they come from? There are two main types of sites in the catacombs. The smaller would be a sort of an arched niche, called an arcosolium, dug into the side of a gallery wall in which several members of a family could be buried. It would, after about 175 CE, be painted with Christian imagery. (Figure 2.)

Figure 2. Catacomb of Peter and Marcelinus: Arcosolium with the Wedding at Cana, etc.

The method of painting used in the catacombs was fresco. Thanks to the intact ruins of the first-century town of Pompeii, we know that Roman artists were very skilled in fresco, and their patrons very ambitious. Sometimes most of the interior walls of a home would be covered by colourful painted mythological scenes, imagined architectural divisions or landscapes. Many of these show strong imaginations and pictorial talents at work. Things look quite different in the catacombs: our breakthrough generation used the same technique, producing more modest and less demanding and less expensive work. The tufa in an arcosolium would be covered with plaster. While it was still wet, the images were painted or drawn on the wet plaster and so bonded with it. It is the same basic technique that Michelangelo used between 1508 and 1512, when he was painting the Ceiling of the Sistine Chapel. The colours used in the catacombs, by contrast, were very limited: usually earth tones like brown and ochre. The lines separating the images in Figure 2 are echoes of the imagined architectural divisions in the current Roman tradition of decoration.

But there were also larger sites in the catacombs for imagery. Rich and important families had burial chambers or cubicula. These were dug out at right angles to the side of a gallery. In one of these, several generations of a family could be buried in loculi cut into walls and floors. The ceilings of such cubicula were often shaped as a shallow dome or vault. Along with the walls, these were often painted. Illustrations of Old Testament stories of deliverance were very popular, especially in the earlier sections of Christian catacombs. Among such stories were Noah emerging from the ark, Jonah saved from the whale and reclining under the gourd tree, and Daniel in the lions' den. (Figure 3.)

Figure 3. Catacomb of St. Callistus. Cubiculum ceiling with, in the centre, Daniel in the Lions' Den.

The earliest Christian paintings in the Roman catacombs (c. 175–225 CE) are a sign of important changes: the Christian community was aware that it was now a visible group among the many religious bodies – home-grown Roman religions and those from the East and Egypt – making up the imperial capital. All of these were polytheistic and could, when required, include in their pantheon the Roman emperors. Christians and Jews, however, who were monotheists, would be in trouble on occasions when they would refuse those parts of the civic rituals that required them to worship as a divinity the Emperor or his image. Such refusals often created martyrs. But in spite of these dangerous moments and several serious persecutions, the Christian community was continually growing because, following Christ, they attracted and welcomed not only the learned and the wealthy, but also the uneducated and the poor.

Toward the end of the second century, Christians in Rome were more numerous: a difficult to ignore 50,000 persons. Their visibility is illustrated by the developments in worship spaces. Up to this time, they had been worshipping in the home, called a titulus, of a usually wealthy believer. But around the end of the second century, some of these ordinary Roman dwellings were being visibly enlarged to accommodate rapidly increasing numbers. The form of the eucharistic liturgy was also developing away from being part of an Agape meal. Now what was needed for the Eucharist was a space with a separate area for the clergy. In this way, the shape of the worshipping space was also changing. Thus the growing presence of the Christians in Rome had become a visible architectural reality. The progression, during this pre-Constantinian period of the Church, was from the titulus, the Church-House; then, probably after renovations, to the House of the Church; then to the usually rectangular Church Hall. Each of these phases was built onto or over the site of the original titulus and, after the freedom of the church in 312 CE and with the patronage of Emperor Constantine (310–337 CE), could be succeeded by a basilica.[5]

The years c. 175 to c. 220 are important dates in the history of Christian art. This is the period when the already richly developing Christian spirituality began to be expressed not just in words but also in architecture and images. Material culture was right in step. It was at this time, for example, that inexpensive, moulded household lamps made of ceramic, bearing Christian clustres of images, were first manufactured for, and distributed and sold to, the emerging Christian market.[6]

It is very hard to imagine that there was a time in Christianity when there was no Christian art. We can thank the breakthrough generation for deciding to get it underway. We can also thank the artist Sarah Hall for taking their efforts seriously and then being inspired by these crucial beginnings.

---

[5]   Archaeology is continually uncovering details of this architectural genealogy of pre-Constantinian Christian buildings by controlled digs under later basilicas. For more information on these fascinating developments, see: L. Michael White, *Building God's House in the Roman World: Architectural Adaptation Among Pagans, Jews, and Christians* (Baltimore (MD): Johns Hopkins University Press, 1990), esp. 102–148.

[6]   Paul Corby Finney in *The Invisible God* illustrated one of these on p. 117 and has an engraving of it on p. 119.

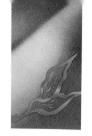

PREFACE

IMAGE, ARCHAEOLOGY AND WONDER

by Sarah Hall

Among the joys associated with creating stained glass for churches, one that stands out is the sense of adventure and possibility that comes with each new commission. You can know everything there is to know about the architecture, the plans, the building committee and the faith tradition, but once these are combined in the creative process, anything can happen. At St. Rose of Lima Parish in Toronto, the unique combination of all these elements led me back almost to my beginnings as a stained glass artist.

I have always been fascinated by archaeology, and just as I consider my stained glass to be a message to the future, I have long been interested in the messages that have come to us from the past, sometimes after being lost to view for millennia. One of the first works I made as a student at Swansea College of Art in Wales was a painted glass roundel of an ancient Celtic figure with arms upraised in prayer. I chose this image because of its honesty and simplicity. It told its story without any subtexts or efforts at realism.

Many years later I was inspired by an art history class at Regis College in Toronto, where I first became aware of the gentle images that had been discovered in the catacombs of Rome. For several years afterwards I carried one of the images about with me – the Blessing of the Loaves.

During my first meeting at Rose of Lima Parish I was struck by the many deep-set windows in the building – windows that reminded me of the catacomb loculus. I was impressed by the diversity of nations represented in the congregation and was reminded of the physical aspect of the catacombs, with their endless interconnecting passages and walls covered in thousands of prayers, earnest requests and inscriptions. All of this bears witness to and resembles the mystical body of Christ.

Out of these feelings and observations came a conviction that the images from the catacombs could be the common thread that united these diverse backgrounds, and that the building itself would be an ideal place to portray these images.

Creating the windows

The creation of these windows combines modern techniques with glass painting traditions that date back over a thousand years. The coloured glass was first created using air-brushed float glass with layers of fired red-gold glass enamels that presaged the shapes of the final design. The particular colour chosen reflected the typical red ochre colour of many of the catacomb wall paintings.

© André Beneteau

I based my glass designs on original catacomb images. Rather than reproduce the original colouration, I reduced the image to a highly contrasting and fragmented black-and-white picture. Working with the fabrication studio we then created a silkscreen, which we used to screen the glass paint onto the coloured glass. I then refined and reworked the screened images through a series of firings that permanently fused the painted images onto the glass.

Similar techniques were used for the small choir windows, which were coloured then fired with reflective gold paint. These echo Christian signs, symbols and decoration from the catacomb walls of Praetextatus.

The windows were created in collaboration with Studio Glasmalerei Peters in Paderborn, Germany. Their excellent facilities and craftsmanship continue a tradition of 100 years of a family-owned glass painting workshop.

Statements of faith

I have been asked why these images are important now. My response is that they have always been important: from the time they were first created, through the many centuries during which they were lost to memory, to their rediscovery beginning in the 1500s, and continuing to the present day. These are simple images, but they are as honest and direct a statement of faith as one can find in any era.

I feel refreshed and sustained by the images of Christ among people at work and doing good in the world: blessing the loaves, turning water to wine, raising his friend from the tomb, teaching and listening to the woman at the well, healing the hemorrhaging woman.

The spirituality and imagery of the catacombs are those of the early church. These images speak to me across the millennia, and from my conversations I believe they touch many others the same way. These are meditative images that evoke the experience of the catacombs themselves, of quiet darkness, of depth, of connectedness to our collective witness and to eternal hope.

INTRODUCTION TO THE REFLECTIONS

by Bob Shantz

Between the second and fourth centuries CE, the Christians of Rome and surrounding cities buried their dead in underground tunnels called catacombs, imitating the burial practices of their Jewish and pagan neighbours. On the anniversaries of the deaths of their loved ones, these Christians would gather in the catacombs to celebrate the life they knew in the one who had died. In these dimly lit places, they were surrounded by paintings that they had commissioned artists to paint on the ceilings, on the walls and even, occasionally, on the floors. It is these paintings that stained glass artist Sarah Hall used as inspiration for the sanctuary windows of St. Rose of Lima Parish in Toronto.

The faith of these early believers is reflected in their art. Their faith is filled with hope for a better life and a gentle regard for the struggles of the present day. We find depictions of people being healed, flood waters subsiding and death being overcome. Women are honoured and Creation is accepted as a great gift and blessing from God. It was not until approximately 1000 CE that Christians began to depict life as a struggle to appease a gracious but ultimately judgmental God. James Stevenson, in *The Catacombs: Life and Death in Early Christianity*, has described the life depicted by the catacomb painters as one lived in the "glad confidence in the love of God." Sarah Hall's renditions of these paintings, it seems to me, inspire in us such glad confidence.

Sarah has faithfully reproduced the essential elements of each painting – no characters were added or taken away. Each image was chosen for its artistic merit and for how it would fit into the context of the sanctuary windows. She coloured each painting with shades of ochre, reminding us that they were painted in the earth and on walls of earth. She has also, intuitively, added light where she felt it needed to be. With these adaptations, Sarah has taken these powerful images from their origins in earth and stone to a new life in the medium of glass, thereby revealing faith, hopes and dreams.

The first time I saw these windows I was immediately drawn to reflect on the stories upon which they are based. Noah came alive for me as a man of action. I was very much taken with the caring and attractive young man, the Good Shepherd. I heard the woman at the well responding to Jesus with her insights. I felt the desperation of the woman seeking to touch the hem of Jesus' garment.

What I have written here is enlivened by these first impressions. I hope that my thoughts will be a catalyst for your own reflections, and that these images will speak to you and guide you in your experience of the gift of life.

Noah and the Ark

(Catacomb of St. Marcellinus & St. Peter, mid-third century, Rome)

This is Noah, the man who gets things done. He and God agree on the terms of a contract: Noah will build an ark and, in turn, God will save him and his family and the creatures of the earth, so that life may go on. This contract is a covenant between two parties who need each other. Noah meets the challenge – he acquires the knowledge and materials required to build a boat on dry land. He then enters the ark and waits for God to be true to God's part of the contract.

Sarah's light falls on the dove, the symbol of the Spirit, which carries the olive branch, the sign of life. Noah raises his arms in joy because he knows that God has honoured the contract. The threat of the rolling and cresting waves has passed. The covenant has been honoured by both parties.

Christians, in the first centuries after Christ, placed great emphasis on their new life, born in the waters of baptism. Surely new life for them would have included the end of Roman persecution – their "flood." These Christian ancestors of ours understood, and longed for, Noah's relief and joy.

Noah, the enterprising one, is sure of himself as he works with God. These are two strong individuals who, in trusting the terms of their covenant, are doing the will of the Spirit. This is a compelling relationship for a fragile early Christian community that is not at all sure of its survival. It is exemplary for us as well, as we fear that our survival is threatened. We, too, must work with the giver of life to get things done, trusting that co-operation – not competition – between species is the guiding, life-giving force.

EMBRACING

Relentless waves
rolling and rising with massive weight,
mindlessly crashing again and again,
moving on to somewhere else,
to someone else.
I could
never have imagined
such complete destruction.
All are gone
except me
and my children's families.
Why me?
Because I could get this boat built.
I was contracted to save life
with this boat.

We saw a sign of new life.
Can I trust to start again?
My children are ready to go on;
they have only begun.
All are gone
except me
and those below,
embracing.

THE GOOD SHEPHERD

(Catacomb of Priscilla, mid-third century, Rome)

Here is a sensitive, kind, gentle young man who loves life and whose relaxed posture speaks of his openness to his world. He is at ease with his youthful strength, still taking it for granted. He is not looking to sanctify Creation to make it more sacred but, rather, is accepting it as the delightful gift it is. The shepherd is at home in Creation, accepting his role as a caretaker, assuming responsibility to care for and protect the world in which he lives.

He is drawn in such a flattering way because he was the one who was deeply loved. Perhaps he was even more cherished because the artist knew he was to die too young. It is a great loss to lose such a beautiful one, resulting in overwhelming grief to the family who loved him and to the community that was beginning to rely on him.

Sarah has placed the light on the sheep, the animal to which the shepherd is gesturing, as if the sheep is receiving acknowledgment for its sacredness. The goat and the birds frame this action with peaceful respectfulness; the animals relax in his presence and seem to be pleased to be with him.

We also want to be comfortable with our world, and want Creation to be at peace with us. In this age of ecological disturbance, our world is justifiably suspicious, even frightened, of us. We must earn its trust. Our integrity as human beings, and our very survival, require that we rediscover respect and honour for our fellow creatures and for our world, in which we live and move and have our being.

COMPLEXITY AND PEACE

The animals are aware of their needs. One is being carried by the shepherd, perhaps because it is tired or injured, or simply because it longs to be held. The sheep to the shepherd's right waits with its head inclined, as if for blessing. The goat to his left has its head raised expectantly. They are still and quiet, trusting the shepherd who is doing his job of caring for them.

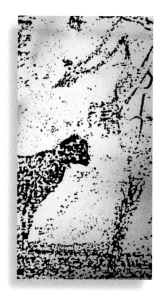

But what is in this young man's bag? He may very well be carrying some bread and cheese, a drink, a flute. Surely he would also be carrying a weapon so that he may protect his flock from the hungry predators that lie in wait.

And what is the bag made of? It is most likely made of sheepskin or goatskin.

A gentle atmosphere of peace pervades the scene. The animals relax, taking advantage of what they have in this moment. The shepherd seems to have learned this from them; he can forget for a short while the disturbing complexity of life and accept this moment as the blessing it is.

Miracle at Cana – Feeding 5,000

(Catacomb of the Jordani of Via Anapo, fourth century, Rome)

Is Jesus here turning water into wine at the wedding in Cana, as recorded in the Gospel of John, or is he multiplying the loaves to feed the 5,000 their evening meal, as told in Matthew's Gospel? Art historians are not sure which is the correct interpretation of this image, but it is clear that in either understanding, Jesus is performing a miracle with his "wonder stick," similar to the one Moses used in the wilderness to bring water from the rock.

Sarah has focused the light on Jesus. He is the one who will transform the water or multiply the loaves, for hospitality must be offered, hunger must be relieved. Jesus is aware of his power to change things. His gesture is not tentative or unsure. Rather, he is intentional and focused, exerting the physical and mental energy required for the task at hand. It takes effort to change things. Effort is expended because the results matter; they are important.

In Matthew's account, the people have come to hear Jesus to have their souls fed with the word of truth and hope. He offers them his Sermon on the Mount. In the evening, their bodies must also be fed. Jesus sanctifies their physical need by multiplying the food at hand.

At the wedding, water must be turned into wine to ensure the "success" of the wedding feast. There must be enough wine to offer appropriate hospitality. This wedding feast must be well celebrated so that the bride and groom know they are truly supported by the community, and so that the community is strengthened by a couple that values its communal identity. In the wedding feast, the couple and the community need to hear each other say, "You are of immense value to me."

In both stories, the community and its members are being fed for the sake of life here and now, not for some spiritual life after death. Our bodies as well as our souls need the food that satisfies our hunger and inspires our celebration.

THE TREE OF LIFE

At the beginning of time, in the book of Genesis, those "who take of the tree of life and eat will live forever." (Genesis 3:22) And in the book of Revelation, at the end of time, "The leaves of the tree were for the healing of the nations." (Revelation 22:2) In the world where the tree of life grows, time is not confined to one moment following the next. Water pours from a rock, the best wine is made from water, and life is born from death. In this world, integrity

is practised even at the price of worldly success, and truth, seen through the eyes of poverty and illness, is valued. Here people rely on faith more than on certainty.

The stick in Jesus' hand is made of the wood of the tree of life. Its power, in the hands of those courageous enough to use it, is a reminder that there is always more to life than can possibly be known. To access the potency of the stick requires that one risk entering and embracing the contradictory world in which the tree is rooted. Everyone has access to the stick, most everyone has used it, and those who have wielded it are fearful of touching it again.

Jesus and the Woman at the Well

(New Catacomb of the Via Latina, mid-fourth century, Rome)

Sarah's light highlights the space between Jesus and the woman, who is drawing on the line that reaches down to the water, making life-giving water available to him. He is speaking with her in a way that satisfies her thirst for meaning, understanding and acceptance. They have an interdependent relationship. Jesus needs this woman to draw out of him his water words of life. As the Messiah he brings peace, healing and hope to those who recognize their need and respond to his presence. Together, Jesus and the woman satisfy each other's thirst.

In the story, Jesus is the "rabbi," the teacher. He teaches not by lecturing, but in conversation where both participants help reveal the truth. His gesture of openness invites the woman to contribute words of truth and life.

He is thoughtfully relating with a woman who is a Samaritan – her people are scorned. In this story, the one who would be excluded from the teachings is included. In their dialogue we learn that things must change for her. Jesus, recognizing this fact, begins to engage her in life-giving conversation. Is this not what we want – for the Spirit to engage us in this way, regardless of who we are? Things must change for us as well, and society must change to allow all people access to conversation that quenches their thirst.

WATER BEARERS

A rope leads down into the well, to the pail that rests in the water as it waits to be drawn up. It is dark at the water's surface; light is weak by the time it comes this far down, but light is not needed here. The rope and the pail know what their purpose is. They wait until the request for action comes to them.

He asks for a drink of water. This is not his well, so she must draw the water up to give to him. The pail rises with its weight of water, trusting the strength of the rope. She grabs the handle and swings the pail clear of the well's wall and pours into the waiting jug.

She offers the jug, sweating with its cool liquid. His lips form around the thick rim and water runs down his chin. He drinks deeply, grateful for this woman and her well.

The pail is dropped carefully back into the well, to splash into the waiting water without touching and bruising the walls of the well, the rope racing down after it. Is this an inglorious end or an ecstatic return to the depths, to the next beginning? The water bearers wait to be called upon again to quench the thirst of one at the surface.

TOUCHING THE HEM OF HIS GARMENT

(Catacomb of St. Marcellinus & St. Peter, late third century, Rome)

The woman's face and posture reveal her desperate need for healing. She has a worried look on her face. She may be thinking, "What will his response be? Will my bold gesture be in vain, or will he stop and respond with healing?" In the story he commends the woman for her faith. It is reassuring to note that her faith is born of her desperation, in her weakness, and this enables her to survive. Faith is a gift of the Spirit for life.

There is a dramatic tension in this image. Jesus' gesture with his left hand is of pulling away, of self-protection, of gathering himself to himself. Is this simply an instinctual response of surprise, of guarding against an entry into personal space? We recognize this humanity in Jesus' response.

At the same time, his right hand is open, stretched out towards her, welcoming her. So often this is our response to the world. We also encounter those begging in the street. We need to protect ourselves from them and, at the same time, we are drawn to respond with compassion. In Jesus we see this union of his humanity and divinity, and catch glimpses of it in ourselves as well.

Things must change. The woman has been hemorrhaging for years and needs healing and ease of life. Sarah's light shines on the woman, suggesting that the woman has seen the power of who Jesus is in his humanity and divinity. She needs to be in touch with this man, even if only with the hem of his garment. She must be in touch with his way of moving through life because then she too can move into the light at the lower right, into the light illuminating the path of life.

TWO SOULS

Two people meet on the street. They recognize the searcher in each other. Both know what it is to be troubled. Both know there must be something more – healing, justice, peace? When two such souls meet, hope is born.

How do they identify the honest seeker in each other? How does she see beyond the apparent strength and satisfaction in him – to see the one who is also seeking with faith and hope and who also at times feels lost and abandoned? How does she know that this is one she can take a risk to reach out to? How does he see beyond her troubling symptoms to the person of faith and hope, to the seeker in her who has not given up on life? How does he know that he should stay, even for a short while, with this one who has initiated the touch?

How do two souls communicate so quickly, at such a deep level, without prior intention and planning? And yet it happens. All the time. Thankfully. When we seek, we need to find. These two found the seeker in each other and their faith was restored. Perhaps that's all we really need to continue the journey with greater energy and confidence and return home in the evening restored, with a story of those we met today.

Raising of Lazarus

(Catacomb of the Jordani, fourth century, Rome)

Jesus' face is grim and determined – death is not to be underestimated or trifled with. In the Gospel of John this raising of Lazarus is the mightiest miracle, the one foreshadowing the resurrection.

Sarah has placed the light around the spot where the "wonder stick" touches the tomb. This is where Jesus' power is focused. She has also placed the light at Lazarus' legs and feet, where the power must reside in Lazarus to enable him to "come out" of the tomb.

Lazarus is small compared to Jesus; he looks like a child in a child's coffin. Jesus, on the other hand, fills the right side of the image. Perhaps the artist is saying that one must be large and powerful to engage with death. Or perhaps the artist wants us to see that life, as realized in the humanity and divinity of Jesus, is always greater than death because such life includes death. Life has taught us that death demands our respect and that life is, indeed, greater than death.

A feeling of resignation lingers here, suggesting that Jesus does not seem keen on working this miracle. There are several possible reasons for this. Unlike so-called faith healers through the ages, Jesus never uses miracles to sway the people, to convince them of his powers. Perhaps this is because it is obvious to him that the lines we draw between the miraculous and the mundane, life and death, sacred and profane, and power and weakness are such misleading demarcations. He must wonder why we do not see this. He knows that no miraculous demonstration in itself will force us to see the truth of our world.

Another explanation for Jesus' resignation is that in his face we can see a weariness resulting from the demands made of him. He must be emotionally exhausted: his good friend Lazarus has just died and Jesus was not there to say goodbye. As well, he has been accused by Lazarus' sister Mary of being negligent. She told him, "If you had been here, my brother would not have died." (John 11:21) Confronting death is difficult at any time, and much more so when one is already exhausted.

There may be a third reason for his hesitancy. Did Jesus really want to raise Lazarus back to life? Would bringing him back be good for Lazarus' family and community? What's done is done; our grieving is designed to help us come to terms with the finality of death. We must wonder as well whether Jesus believed that Lazarus wanted to come back to this life to die again. Jesus knows that we come to resurrected new life *through* death, not by circumventing it. Is he raising Lazarus against his better judgment? If so, does this not reveal his humanity? But his divinity is also demonstrated in his responding with compassion to the pain of those who are grieving. Humanity and divinity are here at one, with great power.

"Lazarus, come out!"

Lazarus is dead.
Family and friends
are exhausted by grief.
Their mourning continues past
the ritual goodbye.
"Give him, give us, new life!"
is their wild cry.
Surely a tomb cannot be a womb.
The tomb is dry,
dark and silent.
No faint light through a moist membrane.
No heartbeat, no distant lullaby.
Do not ask for hope here.
Do not offer hope here.
But do command him.
Cry out to him.
With great force
and great strength
and faith
stones can be moved.

FIGURE AT PRAYER

(Fourth-century painting on the floor of Domus Ecclesia, Rome)

This woman is standing in prayer, opening herself to God. Her mouth is closed and her face and eyes are averted from the one being addressed. She is offering up what weighs on her heart, what must be brought forward but cannot be put into words. Something in her life must change. As human beings we offer up our hopes and dreams, those things that are larger than we are, that are beyond our control, even beyond our imagining. What else is left to do? Everyone comes to this point, perhaps suggesting that this offering up is a defining characteristic of what it means to be human.

In her prayer she seems to be stepping forward, not looking at where she is going because there is only one way to go: into the unknown of the one being addressed. This step is the fundamental act of faith. Our greatest act of faith occurs when we have come to the end of our resources and still take a step into life.

Sarah's light is not focused directly on the woman, but rather on her side, illuminating her right arm and upper right side and face. She seems to be shying away from the light; her eyes are closed. The light of truth is intense; one cannot look directly on the face of God. But as she steps forward, the light seems to be coming to meet her, responding to her faith.

Woman Praying

Her congregation has asked her to stand and lead the prayers. Her posture reveals her humility before her people and before the one being addressed by their prayers. Humility, because it is born of self-acceptance and courage, is essential for praying with integrity.

She probably does not know that her body has begun the prayers before she speaks her first word. Her hands have acknowledged that we live in two worlds. She raises her left hand with its palm up; the fingers are relaxed, prepared to receive. This is the gesture that speaks of having experienced the gift of love. But the splayed, tense fingers of her right hand reveal the other reality that she has experienced – a world of awkwardness and anguish where love has been withheld.

By holding out both hands, she knows intuitively that the full truth of her life is told in both her joy and her sorrow. She still looks to her left, away from the pain. Who can blame her for doing so? Her right hand, however, remains in the light, reminding the community gathered that life-giving truth is found in all of life.

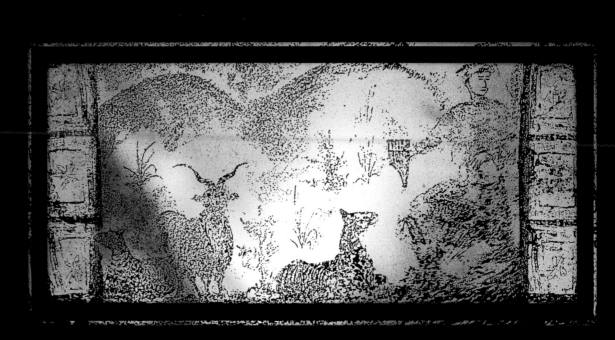

ORPHEUS – CHRIST WITH ANIMALS

(Catacomb of the Domitilla, third century, Rome)

The animals lie and stand quietly in his presence, at ease in the presence of this Good Shepherd. The air is filled with calm expectancy; the music is about to begin. They recognize and trust this man who brings divinely soothing sound.

Sarah's light seems to radiate from the Shepherd's flute. It is a source of the light, shedding light, as a lantern would, down toward the animals. Music is a source of light for us as well. Can we sit quietly, as the animals do, even with our grief and anxiety, or joy, and wait for the choir's music to begin and for the windows to sing to us with their colours and stories?

Church musicians, and all artists, including Sarah, know of the power of the arts to reconnect us with mystery, truth, beauty and peace beyond understanding.

When artists follow their call to express the truth and beauty of our world as they see it, then we must trust that they are following the call of the Spirit. We can be assured that this call does not allow for propaganda or advertising, and it does not resort to sentimentality.

Through the work of the ministry of our artists, the Good Shepherd is offering his music to those who are willing to listen, to those who have ears to hear.

The Offering

The artist creates a work of art to be released into the world. If she is to be true to her calling, she has no choice but to create something and let it go. Expression is not a luxury – it is a necessity.

It is the end of the day, or perhaps siesta time. The shepherd offers the flute, his music, to the animals. But they cannot eat or drink the music and it will not protect them. So why would he do this? Because that is what a musician does. He plays the music not knowing if it will be heard. All he can do is offer.

Religious truths are presented in the same way. There is no guarantee that they will be accepted or even heard. But ask children who God is and, if they have heard a song of love, they will respond with a song of faith and hope. Expression is not a luxury – it is a necessity.

EUCHARIST

*(Catacomb of St. Callixtus, Chapel of the Sacraments,
first half of the third century, Rome)*

The disciples have been travelling together for several years now, walking from town to town, following their teacher. There have been times of conversation, resulting in profound spiritual insight; there have been times of self-doubt, anxiety and fear. Always, of course, there were the day-to-day challenges of where they would sleep and what they would eat. They became a little community. Their followers would begin to refer to them as the church, the family of God.

In this image we see them at dinner. There are plates and bowls of food and drink in front of them on a round table. We know conversation is easier in the round, and we know that one of the most deeply spiritual exchanges occurred at this meal. Jesus said to them that they were to eat and drink in remembrance of him. When they do so, they become one with him, reflecting the union of his humanity and divinity. This is food for the body and the soul.

Each disciple has come to the table with his own thoughts, concerns, hopes and dreams, but at this table he is not alone. They are seated so close together that they must find the trust of one another to be able to relax in their physical intimacy. This is time to pause, rest and enjoy their food in a comfortable place where conversation and silence are honoured and appreciated.

We also long for such times in our own families and communities. It is on these occasions that we sense the presence of the Spirit in our midst. The food indeed becomes a sign of the presence of God – a sacrament – feeding us for the journey through life.

But every family and every community includes members who feel separated from this intimacy. Sarah's light illustrates this sense of isolation. Only five of the six disciples sit in the light. One sits in relative darkness. Is this Judas or doubting Thomas or one of us who, for whatever reason, is feeling set apart? Sarah has given us a profound reminder that remembering Jesus requires that we also be mindful of those in our own families and communities who feel left out.

SPEAK WITH AUTHORITY

Dedicated students get lost in thoughtful reflection with each new lesson. They do not see, and are not expected to see, the big picture. They follow the teacher, who has tapped their interests and abilities and who has earned and honoured their trust. Consciously and subconsciously, they observe how the teacher lives with knowledge, using this behaviour as a model.

But the wise teacher knows that student life must end. One may want to be a student for the whole of one's life, but at some point one must give away what one has received. The student must assume the role of teacher. Such a teacher also knows that teachers, too, need to move on and become students again. They give away who they are, die to whom they are, so that they may live.

Jesus said to his disciples, "When you eat and drink this bread and wine we become as one." When they had finished eating he had become a student of the life and the death that awaited him; they were now teachers commissioned to speak with authority.

SARAH HALL, RCA

Sarah Hall is one of North America's most celebrated stained glass artists. She earned her Diploma in the Architectural Glass Program at Swansea College of Art, Wales, and upon completion spent a year in Jerusalem studying Middle Eastern techniques in glass. Her work has received several International First Place Awards for outstanding liturgical art from the Interfaith Forum on Religion and the magazines *Art & Architecture* and *Ministry and Liturgy*.

In 2002 she was elected into membership of the Royal Canadian Academy of Art and in 2004 received a national award for Leading Women: Arts & Culture in recognition of her leadership in Christian visual arts.

Past projects include the 3,000-square-foot window wall at St. Andrew Church, Columbus, Ohio; the World Youth Day Headquarters in Köln, Germany; and the main foyer window at the Kuwait Embassy in Ottawa.

Sarah's book *The Color of Light* (Chicago: LTP, 1999) is the first book of its kind for the field of stained glass: a resource guide for those commissioning stained glass for a place of worship.

© Malcom Taylor

BOB SHANTZ

Bob Shantz is a pastor in the Evangelical Lutheran Church in Canada. He has served two parishes, and for 17 years he was a chaplain to the University of Toronto, where he was the Coordinator of the multi-faith chaplaincy services. With St. Stephen-in-the-Fields Anglican Church in Toronto, he co-hosted a Sunday afternoon worship service, "Art and the Spirit," to which a different artist was invited each week. A rich diversity of dancers, singers, musicians, storytellers, painters and stained glass artists inspired the congregation with their art. It was at one of these services where Bob met Sarah Hall.

© Anka Czudec / Studio Anka

PETER LARISEY

Peter Larisey, s.j., is from Nova Scotia, where he studied at Saint Mary's University and at the Nova Scotia College of Art. After his ordination in 1965, he received a doctorate in the History of Modern Art at Columbia University, New York. At Regis College, the Jesuit Theology Faculty at the University of Toronto, he lectures on the relationships between Religion and Art.

In his courses students can study both the arts of the Christian period and also the ways works of art of the modern and contemporary worlds have been and are religious. Larisey's study of the artistic and spiritual development of Lawren S. Harris, *Light for a Cold Land*, was, in 1994, short-listed for the Governor General's award for non-fiction. At present he is writing a book whose working title is *The Persistent Spirit: Religion in Modern and Contemporary Art.*

© Moussa Fadoul, s.j.

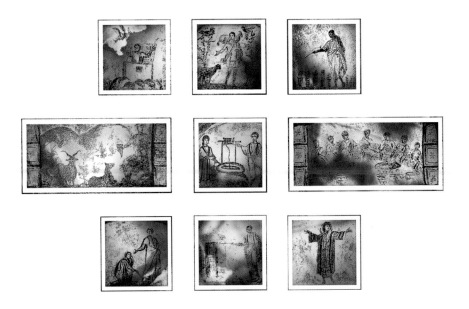

Sarah Hall's catacomb windows have been installed at

St. Rose of Lima Parish, 3216 Lawrence Avenue East,
Toronto, Ontario, Canada M1H 1A4.

Please call the church for viewing time availability:
416-438-6729